Mind Over Marathon

Mental Strategies for Athletic Performance

Table of Contents

Chapter 1. Introduction

Unleash your untapped inner potential with our enlightening Special Report - "Mind Over Marathon: Mental Strategies for Athletic Performance". This insightful guide is a testament to the power of the mind in transcending physical boundaries, transforming ordinary athletes into extraordinary performers. Our report dives deep into the psychology of sports, equipping you with scientifically-backed mental strategies to revolutionize your training approach and race-time performance. Embark on an exhilarating journey, as we decipher the code to mental toughness and sustained motivation, demystifying the art of pushing your limits to achieve your athletic dreams. Harness the power of mind over marathon, for here lies the secret to elevating your performance from average to astounding. Dive in, explore, experiment, and be ready to let your mind steer you towards unprecedented achievements in your athletic pursuits!

Chapter 2. The Psychology of Winning: Understanding the Athletic Mindset

People often perceive sports as a test of physical prowess. Yes, the physical part is significant, but it's just the tip of the iceberg. Deeper under the surface, there lies a wide expanse of mental elements that play an equal, if not far more profound, role in defining a player's performance. The psychology of winning, therefore, is a comprehensive investigation into the mental gear of athletes, unlocking the doors to the mindsets that fuel winning streaks.

2.1. The Importance of Mental Strength in Athletics

In the world of sports, mental toughness is just as crucial as physical strength. Some professionals would even argue it to be of paramount significance. The mind is the athlete's Operating Centre - it governs every movement, every decision. A finely-tuned mental state can foster unprecedented feats of athletic performance, while an unstable or unfocused mentality can tarnish even the most physically fit athletes.

Athletic performance isn't just about what the body can do, it's about how the mind controls, determines, and limits what the body can achieve. A mind trained for victory can push the body beyond apparent thresholds, conjuring a performance that seems to defy the laws of physics. On the contrary, a defeatist mentality can stifle performance, no matter how well-equipped the body may be.

Mental fitness is thus not a secondary consideration – it's an essential complement to physical training. The notion that an athlete's mind needs as much conditioning as their body is not a modern phenomenon; an old Latin quote from Juvenal states, "Mens sana in corpore sano" – a sound mind in a healthy body.

2.2. The Winner's Mindset

Every successful athlete has a unique, personalized approach towards their same general winning mindset. The fundamental constituents of such a mindset usually include self-belief, motivation, patience, discipline, and tenacity. When these elements are thoughtfully incorporated into an athlete's psychology, they tend to shape a formidable competitor.

The foundation of a winning mindset is self-belief – the firm conviction in one's abilities and potential. The winners always consider themselves capable and potent enough to triumph, regardless of the circumstances. Their performance isn't predicated on their past achievements or failures. Instead, winners operate on a 'clean slate' notion, treating each new opportunity as a standalone event with its unique demands and possibilities.

Sure, self-belief can sometimes be perceived as hubris or overconfidence, but it's this belief that incites winners to step out of their comfort zone, challenge their limits, and outperform their counterparts. The insecurities and doubts that can hinder performance are rendered powerless in the face of unwavering self-belief.

2.3. Developing Mental Toughness

Mental toughness is a skill, and it can be honed. Athletes looking to boost their mental strength can work on the following strategies:

1. Goal Setting: Clear, actionable, and achievable objectives give athletes a purpose, a target to strive for. Goals should be SMART –

Specific, Measurable, Achievable, Relevant and Timely.

2. Stress Management: Athletics are rife with stress-inducing elements. Competent stress management is essential, allowing athletes to keep composure during high-pressure situations. Techniques like deep breathing, visualization, and meditative practices can successfully curtail stress levels.

3. Emotional Intelligence: The ability to identify and manage emotions can improve decision-making and responsiveness in sports. Athletes should train themselves to recognize their emotional triggers and to respond appropriately.

4. Resilience: The capacity to bounce back from setbacks is a characteristic feature of mentally tough athletes. A bad performance or unforeseen challenge shouldn't diminish an athlete's motivation or self-belief.

2.4. Conditioning the Mind for Victory

So, how does one condition their mind to adopt a 'winner's mindset'? It starts with changing one's mental dialogue, the internal self-talk that shapes perceptions and response patterns. Positive affirmations can dramatically alter an athlete's mental dialogue, replacing doubts with self-assured statements of strength and success.

Next, athletes should work on focusing techniques to keep the mind's wandering tendencies in check. Techniques like mindfulness and meditation can help athletes garner laser-focused attention, a skill that proves handy during competition.

Lastly, the consumption of success stories – life anecdotes of athletes and their indomitable spirit can be a source of inspiration, fostering a winning mentality. Humans tend to resonate with storytelling, making it an efficient way to promote a positive mindset.

Winning doesn't commence on the track, field, or court; it begins in the mind. The psychology of winning underlines the importance of mental conditioning in athletics, further cementing the crucial role the mind plays in shaping athletic performance. Control the mind, and the body will follow, transforming an average athlete into an extraordinary one.

Chapter 3. Building Mental Toughness: Strategies and Techniques

Building mental toughness, commonly referred to as 'grit', is central to elevating an athlete's performance level. However, mental toughness isn't necessarily innate or naturally occurring in most individuals. It can be cultivated and improved with strategic training.

To be mentally tough is to resist the urge to give up in the face of failure, to maintain focus and determination in pursuit of one's goals, and to endure through challenging circumstances. This isn't a myth or an abstract concept - it's a tangible trait that every athlete can develop.

3.1. Understanding Mental Toughness

Before discussing strategies to build mental toughness, it is important to first establish a clear understanding of what it involves. In the broadest possible terms, mental toughness pertains to an athlete's ability to perform at their highest potential under stress and pressure. It comprises a set of attributes that allow people to handle difficult situations, such as perseverance, resilience, and determination.

Scientifically, mental toughness is believed to be a combination of inherent characteristics and skills that can be learned and developed. It involves various elements like confidence, commitment, control, and challenge.

1. **Confidence**: Having faith in your ability to perform well is a vital

aspect of mental toughness. Confidence lets an athlete face tough situations without undue fear of failure.

2. **Commitment**: Being committed means setting long-term goals and showing the tenacity and determination to follow through.

3. **Control**: Having a good grasp of life outside sports helps athletes control their emotional and mental state, allowing them to perform well during high-stress events.

4. **Challenge** There is an appetite to embrace challenges rather than viewing them as threats.

3.2. Techniques to Build Mental Toughness

Building mental toughness requires consistent practice and a toolbox of strategies. Here are several techniques to consider:

1. **Goal Setting**: Establishing both long-term and short-term goals helps to maintain focus and perseverance. The more specific, realistic, and measurable your goals, the better. Regular reviews and adjustments keep these goals fresh and compelling.

2. **Positive Self-Talk**: This is one of the most widespread techniques for improving mental toughness. Harnessing your internal dialogue can help boost confidence, decrease stress and anxiety, increase motivation, and improve performance.

3. **Visualization**: Another powerful tool at your disposal is the technique of mental imagery or visualization. Research indicates that imagining the processes and outcomes of an event can prepare your brain to achieve the actual results.

4. **Mindfulness Training**: Mindfulness exposes you to your weaknesses, allowing you to acknowledge and address them without judgment. A combination of meditation, Yoga and awareness exercises can help cultivate mindfulness.

3.3. Developing Resilience

Resilience refers to an individual's ability to bounce back from setbacks, adapt to change, and keep going in the face of adversity.

1. **Embrace Challenges**: Accept that setbacks are a part of the growth process. Instead of avoiding challenges, treating them as opportunities to learn.

2. **Change Perspective**: How you interpret adversity directly impacts your resilience. Try to consider obstacles as detours leading you to your goals, rather than roadblocks stopping you.

3.4. Cultivating a Growth Mindset

Developing a growth mindset involves changing how you view intelligence and abilities. Those with a growth mindset believe that intelligence and talents can be developed over time with effort, learning, and persistence. They view mistakes as learning opportunities, which helps them keep going despite setbacks.

3.5. Regular Exercise and Adequate Rest

Regular physical activity can help develop mental toughness, as it naturally places our bodies and minds under stress. Ensuring that you rest well is also crucial; studies have shown that regular sleep impacts various cognitive functions, which in turn help in creating mental toughness.

To conclude, building mental toughness isn't an overnight process. It requires focused efforts, but the rewards outweigh the sacrifices. The strategies, techniques, and exercises mentioned above are designed to assist you in developing resilience, honing determination, maintaining focus, and building the mental edge needed to succeed.

As you continue to train your mind, you'll find yourself reaching new heights, unlocking your true potential, and becoming the athlete you desire to be.

Chapter 4. Goal Setting: A Roadmap to Athletic Success

Understanding the importance of setting goals cannot be overstated. Particularly in the realm of sports and endurance activities, goal setting is a critical factor that can dictate success - or a lack thereof.

4.1. The Power of Goals

Goals provide a sense of purpose and direction, guiding athletes to stay motivated and remain focused on their training. They help transform intangible desires into tangible targets, thus providing a roadmap to athletic success. More importantly, setting ambitious goals could stretch your abilities and push you to perform beyond your previous limits. This is instrumental in getting you closer to your ultimate aspiration - be it clocking a personal best time, completing a marathon, or securing a position in a podium finish.

However, while the overall concept appears simple enough, setting effective goals and working towards them efficiently isn't always straightforward. Many athletes set unrealistic goals due to lack of proper understanding, thus leading to frustration and disappointment. Therefore, understanding the right technique to set goals is equally important as having them.

4.2. Understanding SMART Goals

Enter the concept of SMART Goals. SMART is an acronym that stands for Specific, Measurable, Achievable, Relevant, and Time-bound.

Specific goals are not vague and give precise details of what you want to achieve. Instead of intending to "get better at running," aim to "shave off 10 minutes from my marathon time."

Measurable goals help track progress and can facilitate motivation. By training to "run a marathon under 3 hours," for example, athletes can assess their improvement and the effectiveness of their training regime.

Achievable goals are realistic, taking into account the athletes' current abilities, resources, and limitations.

Relevant goals align with the larger picture and contribute significantly towards realizing the athletes' overall ambitions.

Time-bound goals are crucial in maintaining urgency and focus. A defined time frame creates a sense of urgency, which in turn motivates the athlete to make consistent progress.

4.3. Setting Performance and Outcome Goals

When setting goals, it's important to distinguish between performance goals and outcome goals.

Outcome goals refer to the eventual result you want to achieve, such as winning a race. They are often dependent on external factors and can be influenced by other competitors' performances.

On the other hand, Performance goals are based on systematically improving personal standards, such as targeting to run a certain distance in a specific time frame. They are entirely under the athlete's control.

Experts often suggest that while having outcome goals can be good for establishing the ultimate ambition, focusing more on performance goals could lead to a more constructive training regime.

4.4. Partitioning Larger Goals into Smaller Targets

Setting smaller, achievable targets that lead to an overarching larger goal has multiple advantages. These smaller achievements act as stepping stones on your journey to success, and can keep motivation levels high.

For instance, if the goal is to run a marathon under 3 hours, start by setting mini targets like running 3 miles under 22 minutes, then 6 miles under 45 minutes, and so on.

Such partitioning of larger goals can help create a sense of progress. Achieving these mini goals can provide an extra dose of encouragement and a confidence boost, vital for tackling more difficult challenges ahead.

Remember: Rome wasn't built in a day. Your athletic dreams won't be realized overnight either. Patience, perseverance, and incremental progress are the names of the game.

4.5. Applying Goal Setting in Training and Competition

Goals should guide both training and competition. Have specific goals for each training session, each week, and for each stage of the competition cycle.

The key is to adjust and reformulate goals based on your progress, successes, and failures. Don't be resistant to modify set targets as and when required.

4.6. Reviewing and Revising Goals

A common mistake many athletes make is setting their goals and forgetting about them until the big day. Goal setting is a dynamic process and should change as the situation demands.

Regular reviews allow for checking whether the set goals still align with your abilities and ambitions. This process also helps in identifying any stumbling blocks and figuring out remedial actions.

In conclusion, goal setting can act as a roadmap to athletic success, paving the way for extraordinary performances. Embrace it, give it the importance it deserves, and watch as your athletic achievements reach newer heights. Prosper in your training, trust the process, and let every step you take draw you closer to becoming an awe-inspiring athlete. Let the power of your mind guide you. Harness the potential of goal-setting in your journey of 'Mind Over Marathon'.

Chapter 5. Developing Self-Belief: Confidence is Key

A fundamental aspect of athletic success lies in the deep psychological reservoir of self-belief. While physical training and conditioning are integral to your athletic preparation, cultivating a strong sense of belief in oneself is the lynchpin that ties your physical prowess to your mental fortitude. This chapter explores the profound influence of self-belief in sports, providing an in-depth examination of how profound confidence can amplify your athletic performance.

5.1. The Philosophy of Self-Belief

Self-belief is far from just a mental faculty; it is a philosophical outlook upon your ability to achieve your ambitions. Framing yourself in a positive and capable light is the crux of self-belbelief—imagining yourself as capable, optimized and poised for success against any odds.

Cultivating self-belief begins with recognizing your potential and acknowledging your skills, strengths, and achievements. This acknowledgment constitutes an essential step in generating confidence, playing a massive role in how you perceive yourself and your capabilities, thereby impacting your performance.

5.2. The Science behind Self-Belief

Understanding the science behind self-belief illuminates its effect on your athletic performance. The psychological concept of self-efficacy, introduced by psychologist Albert Bandura, refers to an individual's belief in their capacity to execute behaviours necessary to attain specific performance standards. In the athletic realm, such self-efficacy beliefs influence your motivation, thought patterns, emotional responses, and ultimately, your sporting performance.

Neural pathway formation is another scientific aspect of self-belief, underpinned by neuroplasticity, the brain's ability to rewire itself by forming new neural connections. Repeated positive self-beliefs and affirmations can forge robust and efficient neural pathways, enabling quicker and more confident responses during athletic performance.

5.3. Strategies to Develop Self-Belief

Several strategies can aid in fostering self-belief. Firstly, engaging in positive self-talk is an effective approach to build confidence. By consciously reaffirming your abilities and potential, you create a positive feedback loop between your belief system and your actions.

Secondly, visualization plays a crucial role in constructing self-belief. Through visualizing success in your mind's eye, you prepare your mind and body for an actual performance, enhancing your belief in your capabilities.

Thirdly, goal setting is a powerful tool in developing self-belief. Setting realistic and measurable goals provides a roadmap for you to follow, with each achieved milestone augmenting your self-belief.

Lastly, learning from failures and setbacks, and turning them into stepping-stones is a valuable strategy. Viewing setbacks not as devastating blows but as opportunities to learn and grow boosts your resilience and belief in yourself, making you stronger for future challenges.

5.4. Nurturing Self-Belief Through Practice

While understanding the importance of self-belief and methods to develop it is crucial, actual gains are made through consistent practice. Repeatedly applying the strategies mentioned above—engaging in positive self-talk, visualization, setting and achieving goals, and learning from setbacks—will solidify your self-belief. Like muscle memory in physical training, self-belief also demands repetition. The more you believe, the more comfortable these mental pathways become, leading to higher confidence and better performance.

5.5. The Impact of Self-Belief on Athletic Performance

Self-belief, when firmly established, profoundly impacts athletic performance. A strong sense of confidence allows for greater resilience in the face of adversity. It enhances focus, determination, and the ability to perform under pressure. It also prompts intrinsic motivation, pushing you to challenge your limits and continually strive for improvement. Notably, self-belief can even mitigate the effects of physical fatigue by promoting a positive attitude and strong mental constitution, allowing you to outlast the punishing demands of a marathon.

5.6. Conclusion

No matter what your athletic pursuit is, developing self-belief is pivotal. The confidence built from this empowering mental strategy will pave the way for you to stretch your limits, overcome obstacles, and achieve your highest athletic potential. By consistently working on your self-belief, you'll break free from the shackles of self-doubt, soar past your limitations, and perceive every hurdle not as a barrier, but as a stepping-stone to greatness. Remember, every step taken in belief is a step towards turning your athletic dreams into reality. Harness the power of self-belief—it's your key to unlocking extraordinary athletic performance.

In the end, believe in yourself, and let your mind steer you towards your unprecedented achievements in your athletic pursuits.

Chapter 6. Conquering Fear of Failure: Embracing the Challenge

Success in athletic arenas does not solely stem from physical training and abilities. The psychological aspects of performance are increasingly being recognized as fundamental in accomplishing extraordinary feats. One such psychological element influencing athletic performance is our fear of failure. Embodied as apprehension, anxiety, or even panic, the fear of failure has the capacity to immobilize an athlete's progression and sabotage budding capabilities.

Fear of failure, while detrimental, is not an unbeatable obstacle. The journey to overcoming it begins by acknowledging its existence, understanding its roots, and developing an actionable plan to surmount it. Equipped with the right strategies and mindset, you can transform this fear into a potent tool for fueling your athletic performance.

6.1. Understanding Fear of Failure

Before embarking on the quest to conquer fear, it is crucial to understand the essence of fear of failure in sports. It often manifests as the fear of underperforming, of disappointing others, or of undermining one's self-image. Athletes may be plagued by thoughts such as, "What if I don't make it?" or "I can't let my coach down." Such fears can propel them into a vicious cycle of self-defeat and reinforce the fear of failure.

Understand that fear itself is not inherently bad. In fact, moderate levels of fear can trigger the fight-or-flight response, sharpening your senses and alerting your mind to the challenge ahead. The key, however, lies in managing and leveraging this fear towards enhancing your performance rather than succumbing to it.

6.2. The Roots of Fear

To conquer fear, we must first explore its roots. Fear of failure often arises from external pressures (expectations from coaches, parents, peers) or internal pressures (self-imposed standards, comparison with other athletes). Society's gravitation towards celebrating winners and overlooking the efforts of those who fall short can perpetuate this fear.

When an athlete ties their worth to their performance, it intensifies the fear of not measuring up. In doing so, they allow their identity to be dictated by their achievements. This becomes problematic when external circumstances, like injuries or poor performance, shatter the inflated self-image, leading to an identity crisis.

6.3. Implementing Fear-Busting Strategies

Embracing your fear of failure and utilizing it as a catalyst for improvement requires a holistic strategy. It begins with self-acceptance, veers towards pursuit of mastery, and necessitates resilience-building techniques.

1. **Self-Acceptance:** Begin by recognizing that it's okay to have fears and doubts. Everyone, including the most successful athletes, has experienced fear of failure at some point. The key is not to let your fears control you. Acknowledge them as part of the process, as an opportunity for growth.

2. **Focus on Mastery:** Shift your focus from outcome-based goals to mastery-based goals. Instead of obsessing over winning, concentrate on mastering your skills, enhancing your strategy,

and improving your times or benchmarks. This shift can alleviate the pressure to win and allow you to enjoy the process of growth.

3. **Embrace Resilience:** Resilience is about facing challenges, absorbing the impact, and bouncing back with increased vigor and determination. Incorporate psychological resilience-building exercises into your training regimen. Techniques like mental imagery, mindfulness, and positive self-talk can help build mental fortitude.

6.4. Redefining Failure

One of the most potent ways to conquer fear of failure is by redefining what failure means to you. Start viewing failure not as a dead-end, but as a stepping stone to success. Every fall is an opportunity to learn, regroup, and come back stronger. When you change your perspective, failure morphs from being an enemy to an ally.

Instill the mindset of "failing forward," understanding that every setback brings you one step closer to your ultimate goal. Embrace such setbacks and use them as springboards to leap towards your greater aspirations.

6.5. Embracing the Challenge

Fear of failure can be transformed into anticipation and excitement for the journey ahead. By seeing each race, each training session as a path to self-improvement rather than as a single must-win event, the fear factor decreases, leaving room for growth and joy.

Overcoming fear of failure doesn't mean eradicating the emotion, but effectively harnessing it to propel you forward. By understanding the roots of your fear, implementing fear-busting strategies, redefining failure, and embracing every challenge, you can shift your mindset from fear to fortitude. Embrace your fear as a companion, one which paves the way toward arduous, yet rewarding athletic feats, illuminating your journey from an ordinary athlete to an extraordinary one.

In the end, it's not just about the finish line, but the courage it took to get there, the fears faced, adversities overcome, and the personal evolution that transpires along the journey. Herein lies the true victory. In the war against fear of failure, your mind is your weapon, resilience your shield, and determination your battle cry. Rise, athlete, for you are greater than your fears, and success is but a marathon away.

Chapter 7. Mind-body Connection: The Crucial Link in Sporting Success

Understanding the intricate link between your mind and body forms the foundational bedrock of sports performance. In essence, physical capability is only half of the equation; mental fortitude fills the other half. The symbiotic relationship between the mind and the body cannot be underestimated; it's time to explore the depths of this profound connection and use it as a driving force to catapult your sporting performance to new heights.

7.1. The Science Behind the Mind-Body Connection

Science's understanding of the mind-body connection provides us with a blueprint to unlock the power of the mind. At a base level, our brain is inextricably tied to our anatomical functioning. Much like a deft puppeteer, the brain controls all the strings that lead to physical movement.

Recent research in psychophysiology – the study of the relationship between the mind (psyche) and body (physiology) – has offered significant insights. The body responds to the way you think, feel, and act. This is often called the "mind-body connection." When you are stressed, anxious, or upset, your body reacts in a way that might tell you something isn't right.

Understanding these scientific underpinnings can enable you to leverage the mind-body connection to your advantage. Through tools such as biofeedback and mental training, athletes can gain more significant control over normally automatic body processes, facilitating superior physical performance.

7.2. Harnessing the Power of the Mind-Body Connection in Sports

Traditionally, the training regimens of athletes have heavily focused on physical conditioning. However, contemporary training philosophies emphasize the need for mental training. This shift has arisen from an increasing understanding of the influential role of the mind in dictating sporting proficiency.

By concentrating on the mental aspect of training, athletes can hone not only their physical skills but also their mental fortitude. Routines such as visualization, goal-setting, stress management, and self-talk have garnered attention in the field of sports psychology for their efficacy in boosting performance.

In essence, the way you think can directly impact the way you perform. This is not merely anecdotal evidence; scientific research continuously underscores the vital grasp of mental constructs on physical performance.

7.3. Visualization: Painting a Mental Picture

Visualization, or mental imagery, is a proven psychological technique used by athletes to enhance performance. It involves creating a mental image or intention of what you want to happen or feel in reality. By visualizing specific movements or outcomes, athletes can set their bodies in motion towards achieving the desired result.

Research confirms that mental practice through visualization can be as effective as physical training. The brain can't distinguish between a vividly imagined experience and a real one. Therefore, by performing mental rehearsals, athletes can program their mind and body to respond optimally during actual performance.

7.4. Goal-Setting: Your Roadmap to Success

Goal-setting is another fundamental aspect of eschewing the mind-body connection towards sporting excellence. By setting clear, measurable, attainable, relevant, and time-based (SMART) goals, athletes can forge a path to sporting success and persist when challenges arise.

Aligning your mind with your body to strive towards a common goal can foster incredible mental and physical resilience. Furthermore, reaching these goals instills a sense of accomplishment that fuels motivation, a key component in maintaining consistent training and optimal performance.

7.5. Stress Management: Maintaining Balance

Athletic performance invariably involves dealing with stress and anxiety. Maintaining a healthy mind-body balance requires effective stress management techniques. Breathing exercises, mindfulness, progressive muscle relaxation, and meditation are just a few strategies athletes can employ to keep their stress levels in check. By calming the mind, the body can operate at its peak potential.

7.6. Self-Talk: The Power of Positive Affirmation

The internal dialogue that an athlete sustains with themselves, known as self-talk, can also significantly influence their performance. Harnessing the power of positive self-talk can improve self-confidence, reduce stress, and improve reaction time under pressure. By directing their internal narrative, athletes can push past what they perceive as their bodily limitations.

The mind-body connection is undoubtedly a critical determinant of sports performance. Integrating mental training techniques into your physical training regimen can bring about significant improvements. The mind's power over the body is not just a theoretical concept; it's a tangible, useful tool. With the right mental training and understanding, you can turn the mind-body connection from a concept into a potent weapon in your athletic arsenal. The key is to maintain balance and develop a consistent regimen that caters to both aspects equally. Above all, mastering the mind-body connection requires practice and patience. By putting in the effort, you are setting a foundation to become not just a better athlete, but ultimately, a better version of yourself.

Chapter 8. Meditation and Visualization Techniques in Sports Training

Meditation and visualization are powerful tools leveraged by successful athletes across the globe to significantly enhance their training and performance. Whether it's visualizing the race track or meditating on their performance, these psychological techniques are crucial elements for any athletes seeking to navigate their physical and mental prowess to new realms of excellence.

8.1. The Essence and Significance of Meditation in Sports Training

Meditation in sports refers to the practice of focused attention and presence of mind. Typically associated with peace, relaxation, and reduced stress levels, meditation can be particularly beneficial for sports athletes. Through the act of meditation, athletes can not only enhance their concentration levels but also foster a deep understanding of their mental reactions to different situations, thereby nurturing mental resilience and emotional sustainability.

One significant benefit of meditation is an improved ability to manage stress. The intense pressure associated with sports often elevates stress hormones, rendering athletes susceptible to negative effects such as impaired cognitive functioning and diminished physical performance. Regular meditation aids in lowering these stress hormones, paving the way for superior concentration, positive mental health, and bolstered physical capabilities.

Breath control, a crucial aspect of meditation, can be leveraged to improve an athlete's physiological functioning. Regular focus on breath patterns can better the lung function, increase breath control during strenuous physical activity, and potentially augment the overall athletic performance.

8.2. Implementing Meditation Practices

Training the mind through meditation, just like physical training, does not happen overnight and requires consistent practice. The following steps provide a foundational process for effective meditation:

1. Find a quiet location free from distractions.

2. Choose a comfortable sitting position.

3. Close your eyes and take slow, deep breaths.

4. Try to clear your mind of all thoughts, focusing solely on your breathing.

5. Practice this routine regularly, ideally daily, starting with a few minutes and gradually extending the duration.

8.3. The Power of Visualization in Sports Training

Visualization, also referred to as guided imagery or mental rehearsal, is another potent tool in the athlete's mental toolbox. It involves the technique of creating a mental image or intention of what you want to happen or feel in reality. Visualization utilizes the brain's neural networks to rehearse the sports specifics in mind, thereby enhancing muscle memory and augmenting sports performance.

Research suggests that the brain interprets these visualized images as real, convincing the body to act accordingly. As such, visualization enables athletes to mentally rehearse their performance, thereby kindling a sense of preparedness and boosting self-confidence in their sports capabilities.

8.4. Techniques for Effective Visualization

Effective visualization extends beyond merely visualizing winning. It's about immersing oneself fully in the action considering all senses - sight, sound, taste, touch, and smell. Here's how athletes can practice visualization:

1. Relax: Sit or lie down comfortably and try to relax your body and mind.

2. Use descriptive language: Engage the senses by describing the surroundings in detail.

3. Be specific: Instead of just visualizing winning, visualize the process - the stance, the movements, the techniques, etc.

4. Include emotions: Feel the jubilation of performing well, the rush of adrenaline, and the satisfaction of achieving your goals.

5. Practice regularly: Like any skill, the more you practice visualization, the better you get at it.

8.5. Combining Meditation and Visualization

Meditation and visualization can be combined for maximized benefits. This combination can fortify mental strength and enhance motor skills, which could provide the competitive edge athletes seek.

To combine these techniques, athletes can incorporate visualization into their meditation sessions. Start by achieving a relaxed state through deep, focused breathing, then transition into visualizing specific sport-related scenarios while maintaining the meditative state. This can deepen the impact of the visualization, as the calm and focused meditative state is conducive to more vivid and detailed imagery.

In conclusion, the journey to pinnacle athletic performance is as much a mental endeavor as it is a physical one. Mastering the techniques of meditation and visualization could be the missing link in transforming a good athlete into an excellent one. By investing time in these mental strategies and fostering the synergy between the mind and body, athletes can unlock their Full Potential, setting the stage for extraordinary performance.

Chapter 9. Positive Affirmations: Rewiring your Mind for Performance Excellence

Positive affirmations are essentially positive phrases or statements used to challenge negative or self-sabotaging thoughts. They can act as catalysts, facilitating mental shifts that can significantly enhance an athlete's performance on the track. Harnessing the power of positive affirmations requires a deep understanding of the mind-body connection, as well as the mechanics of mental rewiring for performance excellence.

9.1. The Science Behind Positive Affirmations

Research suggests that our brains function very similarly to a computational device. Just as a computer relies on programming to carry out tasks efficiently, our minds operate based on neural circuits, dynamically influencing our actions, reactions, and emotions.

Repeatedly telling your brain something positive, like an affirmation, can reshape these neural circuits. Over time, what you tell your mind can manifest in reality. This phenomenon is attributed to the brain's neuroplasticity, its ability to adapt and restructure by forming new neural connections throughout life.

Neuroplasticity introduces the possibility of remodeling your thoughts and rewiring your mind. When we consistently affirm positive messages, activities linked to these affirmations get strengthened and streamlined in our brains. This mechanism is heightened by emotion: the stronger the feelings associated with an affirmation, the stronger the imprints on our neural circuitry, increasing the likelihood of altering behavior and performance.

9.2. Crafting your Positive Affirmations

Positive affirmations are not a one-size-fits-all tool. In fact, the more personalized your affirmations are, the greater the likelihood they will contribute to performance enhancement. Here are some key steps to craft resonating positive affirmations:

1. Write down your limiting beliefs or negative thoughts. For instance, "I'm incapable of completing a marathon."

2. Identify the opposite or a positive alternative for each of your limiting beliefs. This could be: "I'm a powerful, determined athlete capable of running marathons with ease."

3. Convert these positive alternatives into first-person, present tense statements. Such as: "I am a successful marathon runner."

4. Incorporate an emotional component to enhance your connection to the affirmation, for example: "I feel empowered and unstoppable as a successful marathon runner."

9.3. Practicing Positive Affirmations

After crafting your affirmations, it's crucial to integrate them into your daily routine. Consistency is key in making long-lasting changes to your neural circuitry.

The morning, just after waking up, and the evening, right before going to sleep, are particularly effective times. These are the moments when your brain is most susceptible to affirmations due to the increased brain wave activity associated with altered states of consciousness.

Saying your affirmations out loud, writing them down, or visualising them can be helpful methods in enhancing the effectiveness.

9.4. Overcoming Obstacles with Affirmations

In competitive sports, it's common to encounter roadblocks, be it injury, a performance slump, or competition anxiety. During such times, the mind tends to focus on negativity and self-doubts, which can significantly sabotage performance. Therefore, formulating and practicing crisis-specific affirmations can help maintain a positive mindset, improving your chances of swift recovery and getting back on track.

For example, if you're struggling with an injury, your affirmation might be: "Every day, in every way, I'm getting stronger and healthier."

9.5. Affirmations and Visualization: A Powerful Duo

Pairing positive affirmations with visualization techniques creates a powerful mental training tool. Visualization involves creating a mental picture of successfully performing a specific task. When you couple this imagery with your affirmations, your brain starts believing in its capacity to deliver that performance.

By integrating positive affirmations and mental visualization into an everyday routine, you're rewriting the script of your subconscious mind, believing, then performing your way to athletic excellence.

9.6. Reflection and Fine Tuning

Just as physical training requires assessment and adjustments, so too does mental training. Regularly reflect on your progress, your thoughts, actions, and feelings. If an affirmation doesn't seem to resonate, adjust it. Remember, the aim is to create affirmations that serve your unique needs, triggers, and goals.

Positive affirmations, when worked into your daily routine, can significantly enhance your performance by reframing your inner dialogue. Remember, words impact mindsets, and mindsets impact outcomes. Herein lies the real power of positive affirmations: they allow you to take control of your thoughts, and therefore, your actions and results. Feed your mind the "fuel" it needs to propel you, not just across the finish line, but beyond, to places where your limiting beliefs no longer hold power.

Chapter 10. Overcoming Setbacks: The Role of Resilience in Athletic Performance

Setbacks and failures are inevitable hurdles on any athlete's journey. Rather than viewing these obstacles as roadblocks, perceiving them as challenges to overcome, can dramatically transform your athletic performance. This paradigm shift requires resilience – a mental muscle that can be trained, just like the physical muscles in your body. Crucially, resilience not only helps us cope with setbacks, but also springboards us toward greater heights of achievement.

10.1. Understanding Setbacks and Resilience

In sports, as in life, setbacks are inevitable. Injuries, losses, poor performances, and slumps are common hindrances that athletes experience. These setbacks might seem detrimental, but they play a crucial role in an athlete's journey, instigating growth and evolution.

Resilience is the ability to withstand adversity and bounce back from difficult life events. In the context of sports, it refers to the capacity to recover quickly from setbacks, maintaining focus and optimism amidst failure. Studying the psychology of resilience provides a unique perspective on how to utilise setbacks as stepping-stones rather than stumbling blocks.

10.2. The Science of Resilience: Neuroscience and Implications for Athletes

The human brain's role in developing resilience is integral. Neuroscientific studies demonstrate the neuroplasticity of our brains — an ongoing process of reorganization, forming new neuronal connections throughout life. This means our mental faculties, including resilience, are malleable and can be trained, just like physical muscles.

When faced with a setback, the human brain activates the stress response, which includes both mental and physical responses. Persistent stress can activate the hypothalamic-pituitary-adrenal (HPA) axis, leading to prolonged cortisol (stress hormone) release. It can negatively impact performance, emotional well-being, and even physical health.

Resilience training helps in regulating this stress response. It helps us to see setbacks as manageable, thereby reducing cortisol levels and enhancing control and composure during moments of adversity during athletic performance.

10.3. Building Resilience: Strategic Approaches for Athletes

Building resilience is a skill that can be practiced and honed. Here are a few proven strategies:

- **Mental Rehearsal**: One resilience-building technique is 'mental rehearsal' or 'visualization'. Athletes mentally rehearse their performances under different challenging scenarios. This method equips athletes with the capability to remain focused and calm during adverse situations, enhancing performance.

- **Positive Self-Talk**: Resilience is also built by reinforcing positive beliefs about oneself. Positive self-talk works as an internal dialogue that boosts confidence and reduces the stress associated with perceived failure, bolstering an athlete's resilience.

- **Goal Setting**: Setting small, achievable, incremental goals can fuel motivation and develop resilience. These goals act as milestones, keeping athletes motivated during adverse times.

- **Developing Grit**: Grit, defined as passion and perseverance for long-term goals, is an essential component of resilience. High levels of grit can lead to better sporting outcomes by inspiring persistence and determination.

10.4. Tackling Setbacks: Resilience in Action

The real test of resilience is in how you deal with setbacks. Here are ways in which resilience plays its part in overcoming setbacks:

- **Adaptability**: Resilience fosters adaptability. It allows athletes to view setbacks as opportunities to learn and adapt their strategies.

- **Perseverance**: Resilience instills the ability to continue striving towards goals, irrespective of the setbacks.

- **Optimism**: A resilient frame of mind promotes optimism. It helps athletes to view setbacks as temporary and manageable, rather than as insurmountable roadblocks.

- **Self-Efficacy**: Resilience enhances an athlete's belief in their capabilities, bolstering self-efficacy in the face of setbacks.

10.5. Resilience: The Unsung Hero

In essence, resilience is a psychological toolkit that empowers athletes to turn setbacks into springboards for success. It is the unsung hero behind every great sporting triumph, giving athletes the strength to bounce back and exceed their limits time and again. By understanding, nurturing and harnessing resilience, athletes can navigate their journey, not with careful steps designed to avoid failure, but with leaps of faith, embracing failure as a staircase to athletic stardom.

So, build that resilience. Stand tall after every fall. Stride confidently in the face of adversity. And remember, it's not just about crossing the finish line; it's about the journey – the marathons you conquer, one setback at a time.

Chapter 11. Maintaining Motivation: Your Final Sprint towards Athletic Mastery

Motivation, an ethereal internal force within every athlete, is what pushes one beyond humanly barriers and perceptions of possibility. It equips you to face physical discomfort, mental fatigue, and all the other odds that athletic pursuits entail. In the realm of long-distance running, like marathons, motivation plays a strategic role in fueling your strength and resilience, in turn driving exceptional performances.

11.1. The Psychology of Motivation

Running a marathon requires rigorous, intensive training over the weeks, months, or even years leading up to the event. During this training period, maintaining your motivation is vital for ensuring adherence to your exercise regimen. Let's delve into understanding the psychology that fuels this motivation.

Daniel Pink, renowned for his work about human motivation, suggests that drive is stimulated by three crucial elements: autonomy, mastery, and a sense of purpose. In the context of marathon training, these elements translate into creating a structured self-training program (autonomy), honing your running skills continuously (mastery), and having clear, meaningful objectives for running the marathon (purpose).

Understanding your individual motivations and aligning them with these principles can significantly enhance your endurance and resilience, propelling your athletic journey to great heights.

11.2. Goal Setting

Goal setting is a powerful technique that lends focus, direction, and meaning to your training process. These factors augment your motivation levels, encouraging you to overcome hurdles during training. Goals can be varied - for some, it might be completing the marathon within a specific time, for others, it might just be crossing the finish line.

Make your goals SMART: Specific, Measurable, Achievable, Relevant, and Time-bound. Whether it's shaving minutes off your best time or simply completing the race, having SMART goals can maximize your motivation levels.

11.3. Enhancing Self-Belief

Close tandem with goal setting is cultivating belief in your own abilities. Self-efficacy, as termed by psychologist Albert Bandura, is a crucial determinant of task fulfillment. He posited that belief in our capability to execute tasks is as significant as possession of these capabilities in achieving our targets.

Building self-confidence is a matter of mental conditioning. Reflecting on your past accomplishments, visualizing success through mental imagery, positive self-talk, and an optimistic, forgiving approach towards failures can significantly bolster self-belief.

11.4. Reward yourself

Keeping the motivation flame lit during long marathon training can be a daunting task. Rewarding yourself for achieved milestones in your program can add excitement and fun, making the training process less monotonous and more engaging. These rewards can range from a nutritious post-run smoothie, an extra hour of sleep, a favourite movie or book, or even a mini-vacation post-race.

11.5. Embrace the Journey

By adopting a holistic perspective that views your training as not just a physically draining process, but also a journey of self-discovery and personal growth, you can establish a deeper connection with your pursuit. Strive not to view your training merely as a means to an end, but a unique adventure in itself making you stronger, resilient, and more disciplined, thereby fueling your motivation continuously.

11.6. Peer Support and Communities

Finally, surrounding yourself with a supportive network of individuals who share your passion for running can be tremendously beneficial. Running communities can foster a sense of camaraderie and mutual motivation, making the arduous journey of preparing for a marathon much more enjoyable and less daunting.

In conclusion, maintaining motivation through the marathon training process requires a strategic blend of cognitive skills, will-power, and goal-oriented behavior. Harness these strategies as you embark on your training regime and witness your endurance and performance soar like never before, your final sprint toward athletic mastery.

9 798857 165096